Make Your Own Costume Jewelry

© Otto Maier Verlag, Ravensburg, MCMLXIV

All rights reserved

Published MCMLXV by Watson-Guptill Publications, New York, New York
Library of Congress Catalog Card Number 65-21693
Made and printed in The Netherlands
by The Ysel Press, Deventer

Jutta Lammèr

Make Your Own
Costume Jewelry

Watson-Guptill Publications

New York

Contents

Introductory

The Patterns

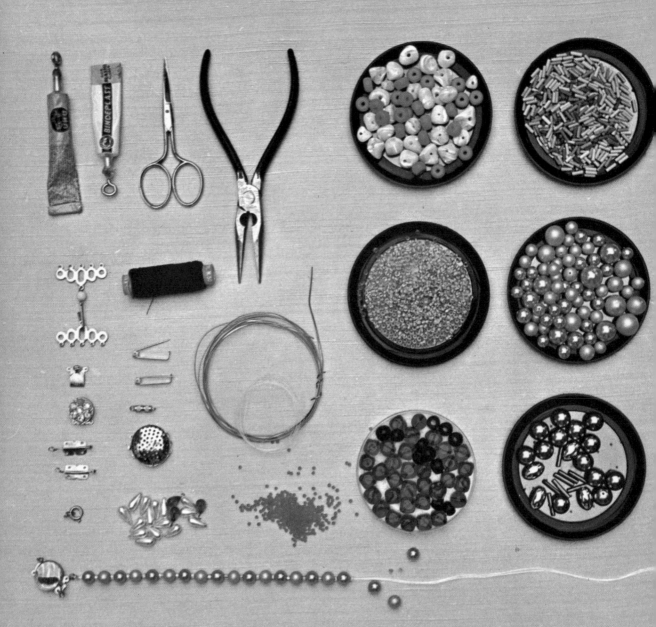

What is costume jewelry?

Costume jewelry has been confused in the past with imitation jewelry, but now it has at last come into its own as a socially acceptable, valued and, in fact, indispensable part of a modern woman's wardrobe. Costume jewelry is not meant to replace or to imitate real jewelry. It is merely one of fashion's frivolities, the modern equivalent of the flowers on grandmama's bonnet, her pretty little lace collars and velvet trimmings: an eye-catching piece of adornment. Costume jewelry is not a status symbol but simply a delight to wearer and beholder. The essence of fashion ornament is to be cheap but not to look it. Hence the importance of choosing the right materials.

Choice of materials

The innumerable varieties of beads can be divided into two main groups: transparent and opaque. They may be made of glass, plastic, china, metal, wood, ceramics and many other materials. It is not so easy as it may seem to combine beads so as to create a harmonious whole. Here are a few hints on how to combine them successfully.

Pale blue transparent beads, whether glass or plastic, combine well with white pearl beads, silver glass beads, silver wire or a silver chain. They should never be combined with copper or brass-coloured materials, which kill the delicate blue. Red or pink transparent beads on the other hand achieve their full effect only when combined with golden tones. However, they also go well with pearl beads (Pattern 13). Combinations of black and white beads would have too cold an effect. The mixture of transparent yellow and red beads, as of red and blue, or brown and green, in equal proportions, is also unfavourable.

You should never use more than two contrasting colours and a neutral colour (silver or gold) in combination unless for a multi-coloured piece like Pattern 11. In multi-coloured jewelry one colour must predominate: otherwise it will look crude and garish. You cannot be too careful in the choice of colours; so much depends on it. The next point to consider is the choice of style.

The various styles

You should distinguish between *multi-stranded* necklaces (Patterns 1 and 5) and *cascade* necklaces—these are also multi-stranded but are made from slender strings of tiny beads (Pattern 9)—and between *collars* (wide or narrow necklaces in which all the strings of beads are connected as in Pattern 16) and *waterfall collars* which are close multi-stranded necklaces with pendant strands or fringes (Pattern 18). There are also many kinds of *combined necklaces:* made of wood with metal (Pattern 17), metal with crystal (Pattern 3), and of metal with pearl beads (Pattern 24).

How to thread

There are two possible methods of combining beads. One may thread them side by side (string them) on *perlon* or *nylon thread* manufactured for the purpose. Alternatively *perlon* or *metal wire* or *elastic cord* may be used. Finally, there is so-called *perlon silk* which is a very fine, almost invisible perlon thread. To use it you need a modiste's needle, which is an extremely fine sewing needle. The perlon thread mentioned above is already fitted with a pointed metal needle-like tip. Perlon or metal wire is firm enough to thread without a needle.

One can also join beads by means of metal links which can be bent (Pattern 15). These links are sections of copper or silver wire which are cut and bent by means of small rounded pliers.

Throughout this book, the British product, perlon, is referred to as the standard stringing material. American readers should bear in mind the U.S. equivalents: nylon thread for light work; metal wire or elastic cord for heavier work.

Fasteners

It is obvious that you need a different fastener for a bracelet than for a multi-stranded necklace. Heavy necklaces need strong fasteners while a light one needs only a simple ring-fastener. The most commonly used fasteners on sale are: *ring-fasteners* (ring and clasp) for light necklaces and bracelets; *hook-and-eye fasteners* for medium-weight necklaces of coarser materials such as china beads; *screw-fasteners*, suitable for all single-row light necklaces, but not for bracelets; *snap* or *push-in fasteners* with several eyelets (consisting of a clasp and bolt with a spring) for multi-stranded necklaces and bracelets.

1 A pretty necklace need not necessarily be of complex design. We start with a simple triple row of blue and white china beads. The beads are the kind used for making table mats. You can buy them from needlework or handicraft shops or even from some toyshops. Get some strong twine (not sewing thread) and either a hook or bolt fastener and you will be ready to start.

First thread the white beads loosely and try out the length; the necklace should hang in a graceful loop. Once the length is fixed, both ends of the thread must be joined to the eyelets of the fastener. The thread is then knotted and threaded back through the beads behind the fastener, knotted once more and sealed with a drop of all-purpose adhesive before the end is cut off.

Now for the second, the pale blue row. The length is known; it is to be six beads longer than the white row. The beads should not be pressed together tightly or the necklace will not hang well. When the ends of the last two rows have been knotted and sealed, the necklace is finished.

Alternative pretty combinations of colours: yellow, orange and red; or pale green, dark green and dark blue.

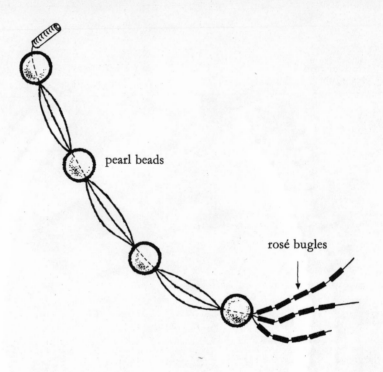

pearl beads

rosé bugles

2 This simple but delightful necklace can be made in half an hour. It is made with three threads worked at the same time. Begin at the screw fastener (a ring will do as well). Knot three perlon threads firmly to the fastener and pass them through a pearl bead.

Thread six rosé bugles (tubular glass beads) on to each of the three strands and then all three again through a pearl bead. Repeat until the necklace is the required length. Finally tie the three ends to the other side of the fastener, pass them back through the grey pearl bead and cut them. Put a drop of clear adhesive at the beginning and end of the necklace and between the last bead and the fastener.

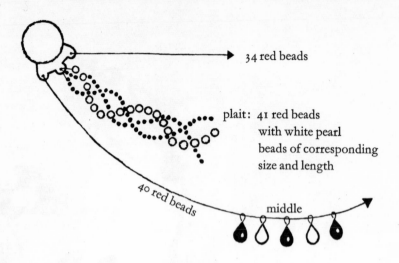

34 red beads

plait: 41 red beads
with white pearl
beads of corresponding
size and length

40 red beads

middle

3

This red and white pattern was made from a discarded long necklace that was fashionable a few years ago.

The red crystal beads are joined by little metal links, but you could simply string the red crystals together with a tiny golden bead between each instead of a link; the effect would be very similar.

To produce this handsome necklace you first make three strings of red beads consisting of 34, 40, and 41 beads. The strings of 34 and 40 beads are then firmly attached to the upper and lower eyelets respectively of a three-eyelet fastener. Next thread two strands of little white pearl beads of the same length as the 41-bead string. Make a loose plait of these three strands, two white and one red, and attach the end of it to the middle eyelets of the push-in fastener. In the middle of the bottom strand of the whole necklace attach three red and two white tear-drop beads which are fitted with little links for hooking. The central plait must not be too tightly plaited so that the necklet may hang gracefully.

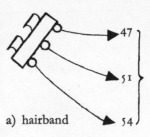

47 ⎫
51 ⎬ plaited beads
54 ⎭

a) hairband

4 This collar necklace and matching hairband of mat-finished and lustrous pearl beads would suit a young girl. It is of pale green beads. Whereas the hairband, consisting of three plaited strands of beads, is threaded on thin elastic cord, the collar requires perlon cord. It consists of a basic inner row of polished beads and two scalloped rows of mat beads, and has an inconspicuous screw-fastener. The sketch shows the exact number of beads in each row to be worked. The hairband is a little coronet to be worn with a formal piled-up or coiled coiffure. If enough material is left over, a bracelet might be worked in the same style. In any case all three ornaments should never be worn at the same time.

16

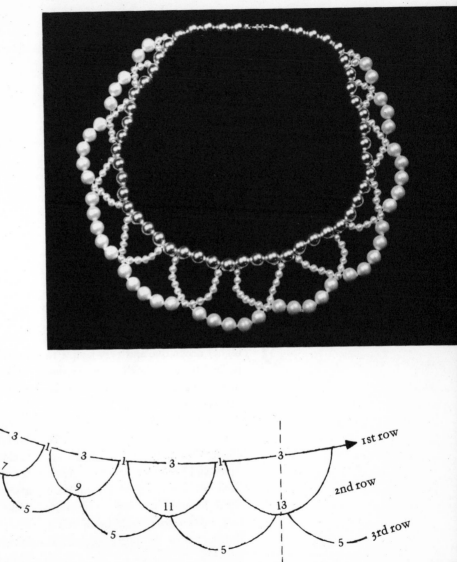

fastener

2nd row

3rd row

1st row

1 · 1 · 2 · 1 · 3 · 1 · 3 · 1 · 3 · 1 · 3 · 1st row

3 · 2 · 5 · 3 · 3 · 3 · 7 · 9 · 11 · 13 · 2nd row

2 · 3 · 5 · 5 · 5 · 5 · 5 · 3rd row

b) necklace

17

5 This amber and gold necklace is highly decorative and very simple to make. It goes with a surprising number of different outfits. You can get the gilded metal chains at a fashion novelty counter if you ask for a chain girdle. They can also be bought by the yard from hardware shops and handicraft suppliers. Apart from the chain, divided into three equal lengths, you will need some long brown-glass bugle beads and a fastener with as many eyelets as possible.

Assuming that your push-in fastener has seven eyelets, you attach a chain to the second, fourth and sixth eyelet. A string of the brown bugles should be attached to the first, third, fifth and seventh. All strands should be approximately the same length to give the necklace its proper thickness. Dark-brown 'crystal' beads may be threaded at intervals among the bugle beads. To make the necklace even fuller, several strands may be attached to each eyelet of the fastener. The thicker it is made the more effective it will be.

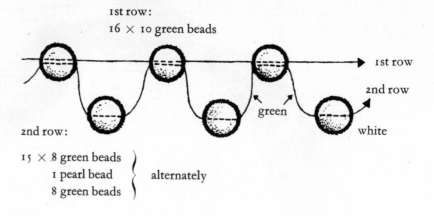

1st row:

16 × 10 green beads

1st row

2nd row

green

white

2nd row:

15 × .8 green beads }
1 pearl bead } alternately
8 green beads }

 For a collar necklace, the little embroidery beads should always be darker than the larger pearl beads. This model is made of transparent dark-green embroidery beads and white pearl beads.

After joining the fine perlon thread (obtainable on a card from needlework and handicraft retailers) to the fastener, thread 10 embroidery beads and then one pearl bead and repeat this 16 times; add 10 more green beads before attaching the thread to the other side of the fastener. Do not cut off the end of the thread but pass it back through the first 10 green beads and the pearl one to begin the scalloped row. It consists of 15 scallops, each with eight green beads, one pearl bead in the centre and another eight green beads. At the end of each loop, the thread is passed through the pearl bead of the original row before the next loop is begun (see sketch). Finally the thread is passed through the last pearl bead of the original row to the fastener, knotted and sealed with adhesive.

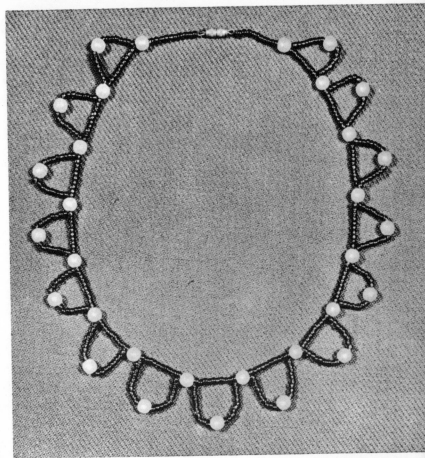

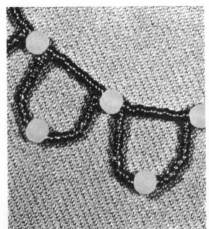

21

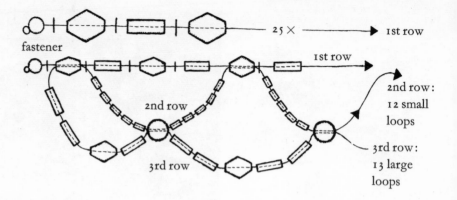

fastener

25 ×   1st row

1st row

2nd row: 12 small loops

3rd row: 13 large loops

2nd row

3rd row

7 Collar necklaces are especially pretty but also the most expensive. It is well worth the trouble to make them yourself. The pattern shown is not difficult to copy.

Starting at the little fastener, thread a paillette (spangle), then a red plastic bead, then a paillette, then a little golden glass bugle; repeat 25 times.

2nd row: Beginning at the fastener again, the thread passes through the paillette, red bead and second paillette before five glass bugles, a pink plastic bead and five more bugles are threaded. The bugle, paillette, red bead, paillette and next bugle of the first row are thus jumped over. The thread now passes through the paillette, the third red bead and the paillette after it. Continue thus to the end of the row.

3rd row: The thread to start this row is knotted, passed through the first red bead behind the fastener and sealed with adhesive. For the first large loop, thread two long brown bugle beads, one red plastic bead and one long brown bugle, and pass the thread through the pink plastic bead of the second row. Continue with 11 loops, each consisting of two brown bugles, one red plastic bead and two more brown bugles. The last loop before the end must be like the first. The end of the thread should be both knotted and sealed with adhesive as with all the patterns given.

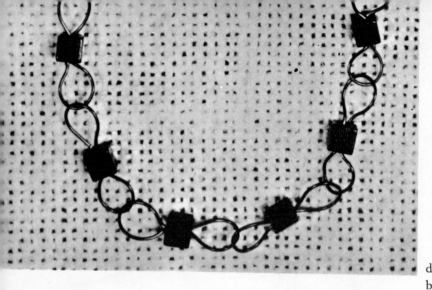

8 Green dice-shaped wooden beads and copper wire are used for this necklace. Its effect depends upon the correct proportioning of the metal and wooden parts.

The metal links are simple to make: sections of copper wire $4/5$ inch long are bent round a pencil, each fitted into a bead and the end bent round the pencil again. So the necklace grows section by section until it is the required length. It is best to make it just long enough to slip over the head so that its pattern need not be broken by the insertion of a fastener.

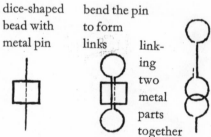

dice-shaped bead with metal pin

bend the pin to form links

linking two metal parts together

No creative talent but a great deal of patience goes to the making of this heavy plaited necklace of tiny embroidery beads. Besides this you will need six boxes of pale blue beads, 10 yards of perlon thread (five cards of the finest thread), and a fairly strong clip-in fastener with three eyelets.

Method: The beads are threaded in

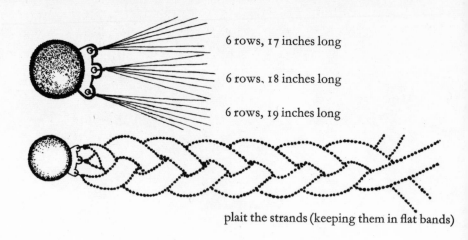

6 rows, 17 inches long

6 rows, 18 inches long

6 rows, 19 inches long

plait the strands (keeping them in flat bands)

18 separate strands as follows:
6 strands 17 inches long
6 strands 18 inches long
6 strands 19 inches long.
Next attach six strands separately and neatly to each eyelet of the fastener and seal them with adhesive. The end must not be cut off until the adhesive has dried. The three bands of six rows are now loosely plaited; the difference in their length will produce the curve of the necklace. The ends of the 18 rows are again separately attached to the eyelets of the fastener. This demands great care (in knotting firmly and applying adhesive), as the completed necklace is fairly heavy.

few larger pink pearl beads. The sketch showing the method of shaping (the pattern of which need not be copied but may be modified) for the sake of clarity shows the shape of the wire as it would be without beads. Begin with the large pearl bead on the left, bend the wire to a flat figure of eight, bend the wire up to the centre in a loop of equal size, then back again to wind it twice round the centre of the half-finished design, as in making a bow. The pendant end of the wire, like the starting end, finishes with a pearl bead, is bent tightly round and pushed into the bead. Now an occasional rosé glass teardrop can be hung here and there as in the photograph. It is quite easy to attach a little brooch fixture to the wire at the back; seal the thread with adhesive.

10 This little shoulder-knot brooch is distinctive and decorative. It is made of copper wire, which is threaded as it is curved with small white and a

fix the pin underneath with adhesive

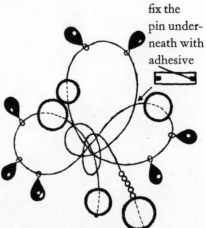

A bracelet of many-coloured transparent droplets can often be worn, as it goes with anything plain, from a simple jumper to a little black suit. The glass-like droplets fitted with little links are quite cheap, and are particularly decorative and easy to use. A simple metal bracelet with even, reasonably large links is the basis. The opened links of the drops are hooked into the links of the chain and closed with little rounded pliers.

The bracelet can contain nearly all the colours of the rainbow but, since the beads are transparent, pale colours should predominate. It is advisable to insert three drops in each eyelet of the fastener to weigh it down so that it stays under the wrist.

11

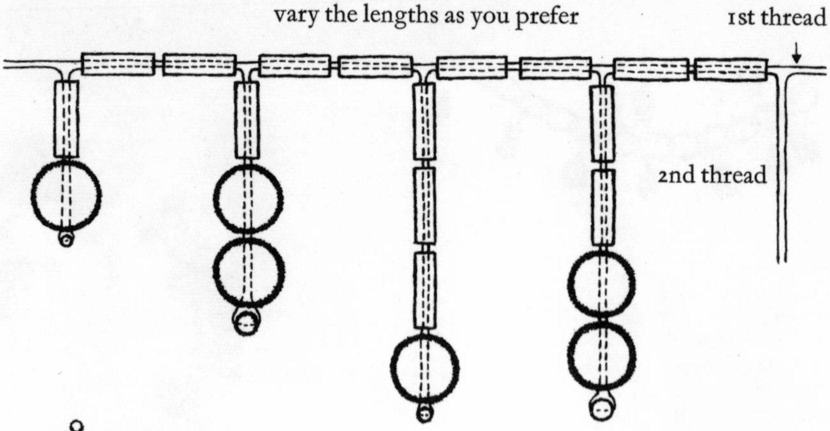

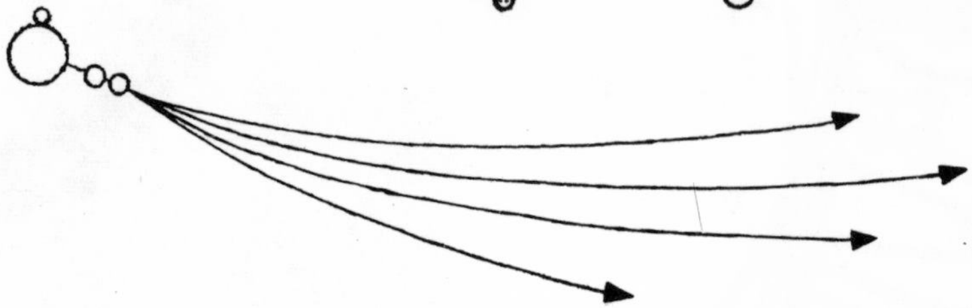

1st thread

2nd thread

12 This necklace of amber glass bugles and 'crystal' plastic or glass beads in varying shades of brown is a real treasure. It is simple to copy.

First thread the long bugles in four separate strands of equal length. You can measure the length for yourself; a collar necklace should not start below the neckline. Attach the four strands to a simple fastener, knot and seal them.

Now, to each of the four circles, attach the fringe, longer or shorter as preferred, consisting of bugles and round beads. Each time, pass the thread through a few of the bugles of the original circle as shown in the sketch.

Resist the temptation to make this model in contrasting colours—a single colour gives it simple elegance.

13

For this pattern you will need about 100 white pearl beads and 17 red plastic beads. Of course, glass ones would do instead but would be heavier and more expensive. First attach the end of a perlon thread firmly to one side of the fastener and thread three foam or pearl beads; now thread five pearl beads and one red plastic bead, repeating this five more times to reach the centre of the necklace. Now prepare the two tassel strands to hang in the centre. On two strands of equal length, thread 11 pearl beads about $\frac{1}{8}$ inch apart. To keep them evenly separated, either make a knot or put a drop of adhesive between each bead. On each of the four ends hang a red plastic bead, knotting and sealing it. By passing the end of the thread back through the red bead already threaded at the centre of the main necklace, form a loop (see sketch) through which the two strands of the tassel can be passed. The second half is worked like the first, with three white beads beside the fastener. Knot the end neatly to the fastener, pass it back through the three beads and seal it. It is not, of course, necessary to use the number of beads suggested. The length of the necklace will depend on the size of the beads.

ring fastener

6 ×   6 ×

hang the tassel
rather irregularly

wind the wire with beads
round a thick pencil

draw the spirals apart

brooch pin

arrange
the spirals
in a rosette
round the
starting bead

perlon threads
strung with beads

It takes barely half an hour to make the brooch on page 35. You need copper wire, medium-size multi-coloured beads, preferably plastic, a brooch pin and adhesive.

Thread the beads on the wire in whatever arrangement you wish. Bend the ends of the section of wire tightly back into the hole of the first and last beads. Take a thick pencil or wooden spoon handle and wind the wire round it several times. Pull the resulting spiral out flat (see sketch). Using the first bead as the centre, form the flat spiral into a rosette. Hang four strands loosely strung with beads to the lower loops of the rosette; at this point the two ends of the wire rosette can be joined to gether. Finally attach the brooch pin to the back with cotton and adhesive. A drop of adhesive applied to each curve of the rosette at the back will keep it in shape.

14

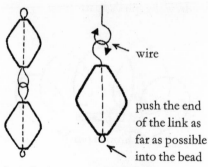

wire

push the end
of the link as
far as possible
into the bead

bracelet hung with linked beads in your own arrangement

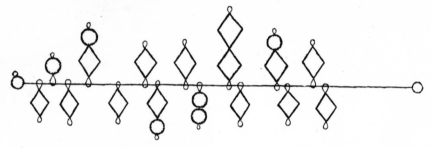

15

Cuff-links can be made not only of transparent plastic but also of wood, china or glass beads. Simply pass a little copper or silver wire pin through the bead, bend one of the ends tightly with small round pliers and push it back as far as possible into the bead.

The other end, a little longer if possible, is bent into a link into which the second bead, prepared in the same way, is hooked. A multi-coloured bracelet can be made by the same process. The basis is a silver or gilt chain with strong, simple links. Into this chain you can hook small and large beads of various colours according to your taste. They are all hung by a link through the centre. The little loop at the end of each bead should be pushed as far in as possible so that it will not catch on your clothes.

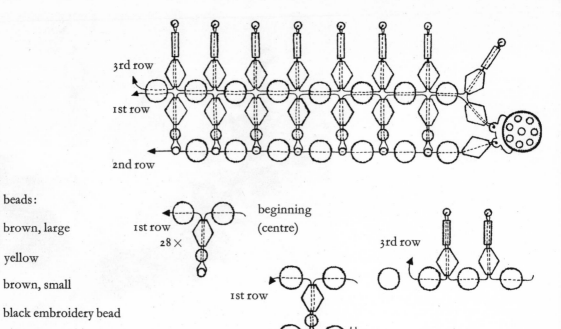

beads:

⬡ brown, large

◯ yellow

○ brown, small

o black embroidery bead

▭ gold bugle

3rd row

1st row

2nd row

1st row 28 ×

beginning (centre)

1st row

2nd row

3rd row

16 This collar consists of very light moulded plastic beads that sparkle gaily. It can be worked on two threads simultaneously, the first and third rows. The second row is worked at the end, and its thread is used to draw the necklet in to the right size. The sketches show the order of threading of the rows. If you find this method too complicated, you can thread the rows one by one. The process may appear complex at first sight but very soon becomes clear when you start work. If you do go wrong, it is easy to undo it and put it right.

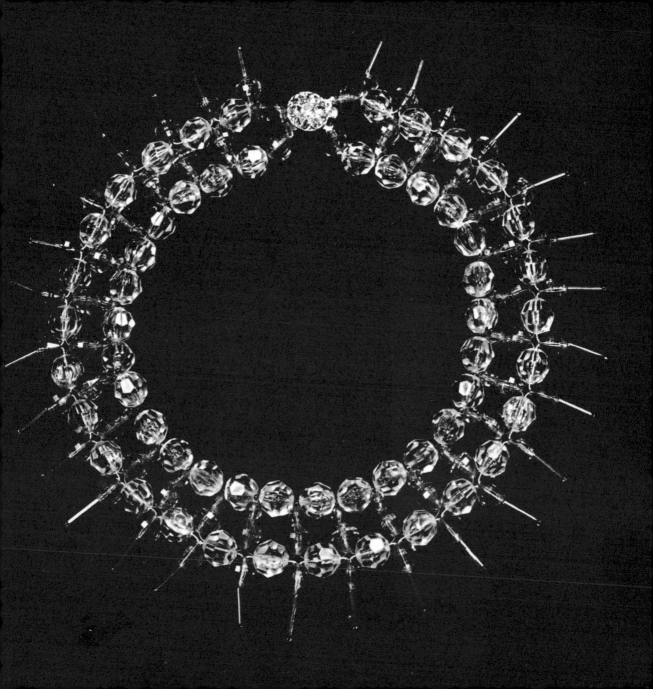

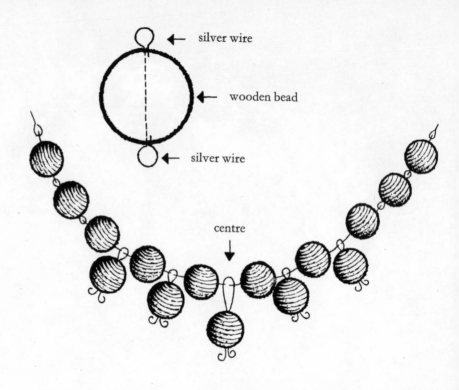

silver wire

wooden bead

silver wire

centre

17 The charm of this simple necklace of teak-coloured wooden beads, the size of cherries, on silver wire lies in the beauty of its materials.

The separation of the beads enhances the effect of their grain. The silver wire links should not be larger than the proportion shown in the photograph and sketch. The pin which passes through each bead should be bent with small round pliers.

The sections are hooked together before the links are completely closed. In the model necklace, five more single beads were hung from the middle, but this addition is optional. The necklace is fitted with a silver screw fastener.

18

This waterfall necklace is styled for evening-dress occasions. Its basis is two plain rows of pearl beads joined by little cross-strands of red embroidery beads. The sketch shows the method.

Through the outer row of pearl beads a row of alternating loops and tassels is threaded. The five middle tassels make the 'waterfall'. These tassels, of

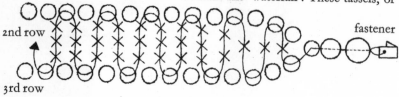

1st row

2nd row

fastener

3rd row

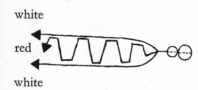

white

red

white

long strands of beads, are added last. To make them, knot the end of a perlon thread about six inches long. Thread a red embroidery bead down to hold on the knot and seal the knot. Make a fresh knot after the bead and push a pearl bead over it and seal it. Continue to thread the pearl beads in this way at intervals of about $\frac{1}{4}$ inch to

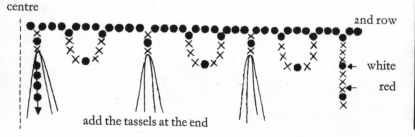

centre

2nd row

white

red

add the tassels at the end

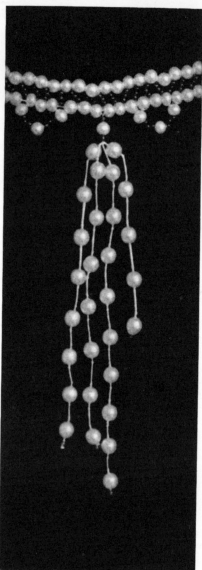

40

the end of the strand, ending with another red embroidery bead on the last knot. Make 10 such strands and attach them in pairs, doubled to hang in irregular lengths from the centre of the necklace.

thread with knot

push the beads over the knots

seal with adhesive

attach   the tassels
in twos

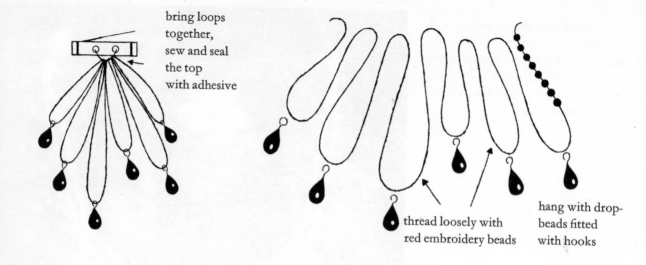

bring loops
together,
sew and seal
the top
with adhesive

thread loosely with
red embroidery beads

hang with drop-
beads fitted
with hooks

19

Parisian women wear these dangle knots pinned to the blouse, the lapel, the waistband or the belt according to their fancy. They cost almost nothing to make. You need a yard of perlon thread, some glowing red transparent embroidery beads, black teardrop beads fitted with hooks and a little brooch-pin. These pins are brass-coloured and have two little holes bored in the bar.

Use an extra fine sewing needle to thread the beads loosely, leaving about four inches of the thread free at each end. These ends are used to tie the bundle of irregular loops together (see sketches). The top must now be firmly sewn and sealed with adhesive to the brooch. To hide the stitches, give a second coat of adhesive and sprinkle it with beads. Finish each loop with a black hooked teardrop.

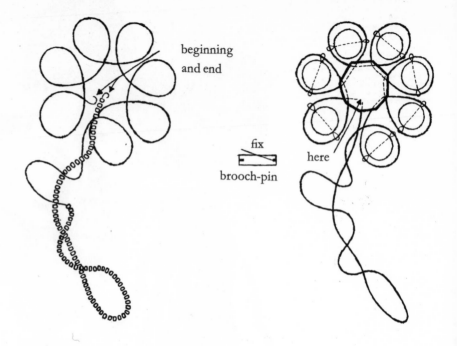

beginning
and end

fix

brooch-pin

here

20 This simple elegant little brooch is made of thin copper wire, red and green embroidery beads, a few pearl beads and a glass button (for the centre). It is very easy and inexpensive to make.

While bending the wire as shown in the sketch, thread it with the tiny beads. Avoid sharp corners in bending as they show the wire between the beads. Naturally you can design your own flower and colour scheme.

The pattern is merely an example of what can be done.

The pearl beads within the petals are sewn in with perlon thread and sealed with adhesive. The glass bead in the centre need only be stuck on with adhesive. It is actually a button to the flat back of which the brooch is attached. It is best to sew and seal the brooch on. Bend the beginning and end of the wire to a hook and link, and join them firmly together.

44

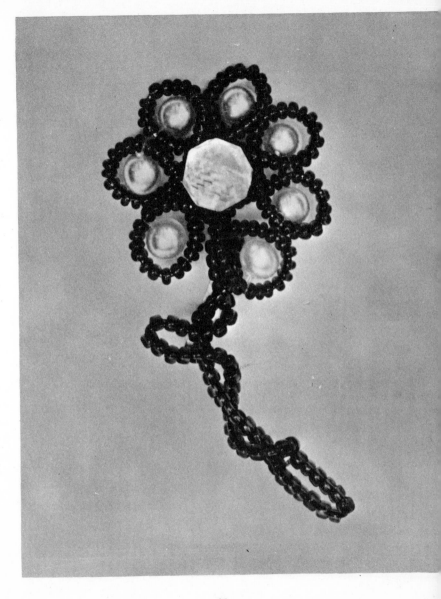

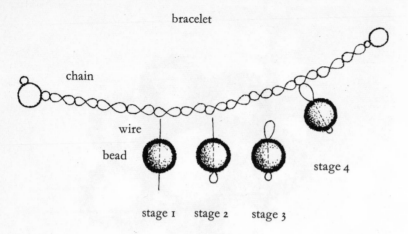

bracelet

chain

wire

bead

stage 1   stage 2   stage 3

stage 4

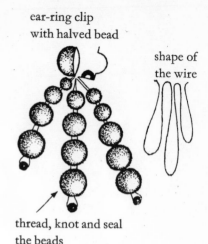

ear-ring clip
with halved bead

shape of
the wire

thread, knot and seal
the beads

21 A set of pearl bead ornaments in three colours is very adaptable.

The bracelet is made like that on page 34. The basis is a simple chain with fairly large links into which the linked beads can be hooked.

The necklace is made as follows: thread the beads in the order shown in the sketch on a thread about two yards long, shortened to the length required and fitted with a push-in fastener. With the remainder of the thread, attach five three-bead pendants to the bottom centre of the necklace as shown in the sketch.

The ends of this thread are knotted twice on each side; each knot is pushed inside a bead and there sealed with adhesive. So that the bottom bead of the pendants may not work off, an embroidery bead is threaded after it before the thread is passed back.

The ear-pendant, which would be

46

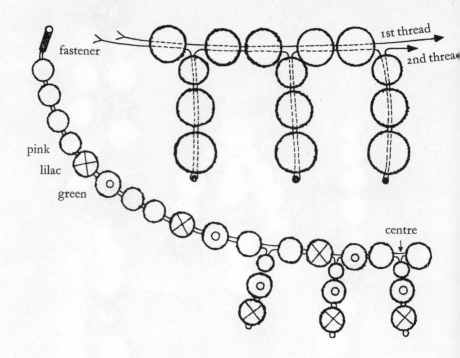

1st thread

2nd thread

pink

lilac

green

centre

equally suitable as a lapel or neckline ornament, is simple to make.

Pendant strands of beads threaded on perlon are tied and sealed to the ear-clip fixture. Saw a large pearl bead in half with a fretsaw or a long narrow-bladed saw and glue it to the outside of the ear-clip. Alternatively attach several small beads to the clip with adhesive or sprinkle it with tiny beads.

48

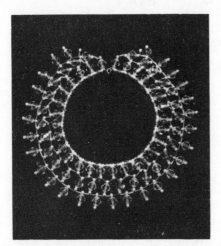

This wide evening necklace is worked to fit the neck closely, like a collar. It is made of large and small light-blue transparent beads, little white pearl beads and silvery white glass bugles. Look at the numerical composition carefully before starting work. From the right-hand side of the sketch (page 50) you can see exactly how each row is composed.

The colour arrangement is as follows:

1st row: two white and a light blue

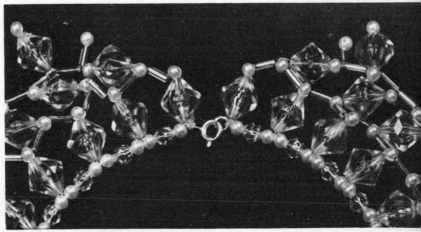

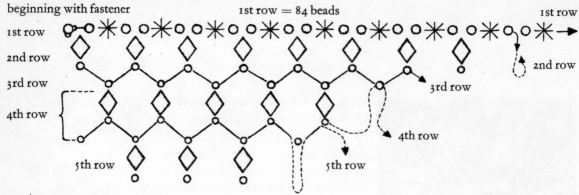

beginning with fastener   1st row = 84 beads   1st row

1st row

2nd row

3rd row

4th row

5th row   5th row

✳ small light-blue bead

○ pearl bead

◇ large light-blue bead

—— bugle

bead alternately. 84 beads in all (average neck measurement).

2nd row: one large light blue and one white bead, hanging between the two white beads of the 1st row.

3rd row: bugle—pearl bead—bugle, each time threaded through the pearl bead of the 2nd row.

4th row: pearl bead—bugle—pearl bead—light blue bead. Then pass the thread through the pearl bead of the 3rd row and pass it back through the light blue and the pearl bead.

Now again: bugle—pearl bead—bugle—pearl bead—light blue bead, etc.

(see start of 4th row).

5th row: attach the light blue and the pearl bead to hang from the pearl bead on the loop of the 4th row. The fifth row completes the collar. The process sounds complicated when described but, in carrying it out, you will find that the successive stages follow one another quite obviously. Consisting entirely of plastic, the necklace is very light. However, be very neat and thorough in knotting and sealing the ends of the threads to the fastener. It is best to use the finest perlon thread.

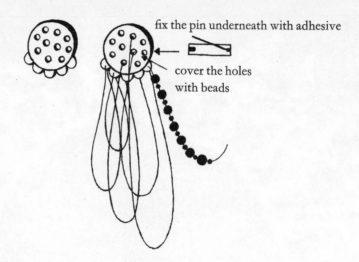

fix the pin underneath with adhesive

cover the holes
with beads

23 The foundation of this brooch is a circular necklace clip, the top of which is bored with little holes. The end-strands of perlon-threaded beads are attached to these holes so that they hang in long loops.

To cover up the innumerable threads and knots on top of the clip, coat it with adhesive and then sprinkle it with the remaining loose beads. Any empty spaces left can be filled with adhesive and single beads inserted with pincers.

Finally attach a simple brooch-pin to the back of the clip with strong adhesive. The join will be permanent if left to dry long enough. All the same, it is best to use plastic beads, the lightest, for this brooch. Suggested colours: orange/brown, red/black, or blue/white. You may prefer to use one colour; the brooch looks smart in black beads.

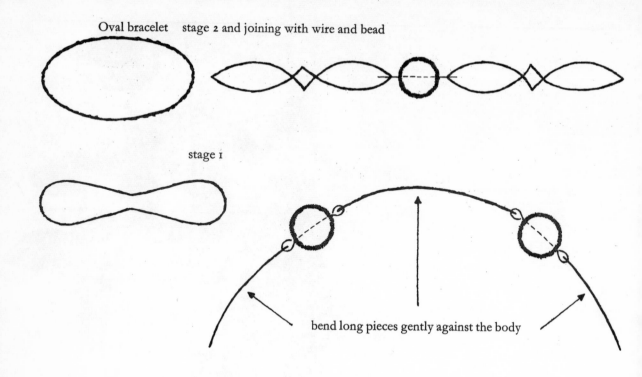

Oval bracelet   stage 2 and joining with wire and bead

stage 1

bend long pieces gently against the body

24 Rose-coloured pearl beads and small children's silvery bracelets are used for this distinctive hand-made necklace. The sketches show the four stages in the bending of the bracelets. A pearl bead threaded with a silver-wire hook and eye links the metal sections together. The ends of the wire are bent, hooked into the metal and then pushed back into the bead with small rounded pliers.

When the necklace is long enough, curve it gently round your waist to shape it. It needs no fastener as it is big enough to slip over the head.

54

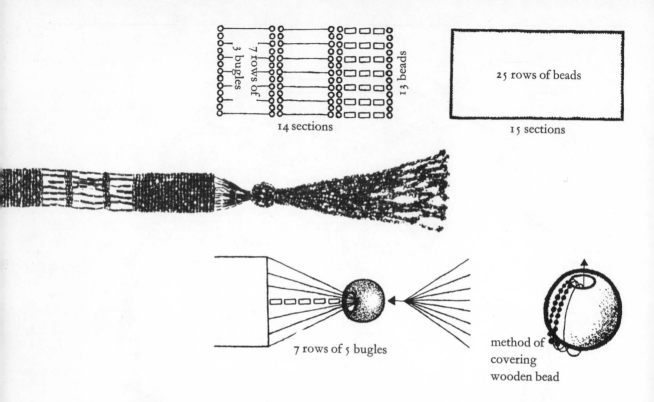

7 rows of 3 bugles

13 beads

14 sections

25 rows of beads

15 sections

7 rows of 5 bugles

method of covering wooden bead

25 The crowning achievement in bead-work is a girdle of tiny embroidery beads. It consists of alternating tightly and loosely strung sections, separately made and joined afterwards to the required length. The model shown has 14 open-work sections of tiny round and bugle beads, and 15 close-strung sections consisting of 25 strands of 13 beads each.

The closed sections are made by a simple weaving process (by which children make bead-mats). The order of the round and bugle beads in the open-work sections is best seen from the sketch. The ends of the girdle can either be ornamented with a tassel and bead-covered wooden bobble or left just as they are, ending with plain sections.